You Do You

Sam Morley

Sam Morley is a poet of Australian/Filipino
heritage. His work has been published by
a number of journals and appeared on noted
shortlists including the ACU Poetry Prize and
the Montreal Poetry Prize. In 2022, he was the
recipient of the Tina Kane Emergent Writer Award
at the Mildura Writer's Festival. His first collection,
Earshot, was published by Puncher & Wattmann
in 2022. Sam has been writing for fifteen years.
He lives in Naarm/Melbourne

Sam Morley

You Do You

UPSWELL

First published in Australia in 2023
by Upswell Publishing
Perth, Western Australia
upswellpublishing.com

ISBN: 978-0-6455368-5-0

NATIONAL LIBRARY OF AUSTRALIA — A catalogue record for this book is available from the National Library of Australia

Cover design by Chil3, Fremantle
Typeset in Foundry Origin by Lasertype

Upswell Publishing is assisted by the State of Western Australia through its funding program for arts and culture.

Department of
Local Government, Sport
and Cultural Industries
GOVERNMENT OF WESTERN AUSTRALIA

To Jordie Albiston
For starting it, for keeping it going

In one stride night then takes the hill
William Stafford

Contents

I've come here for this

Origin story

The first time I was led by a girl
through bracken to a cave
with a view over stony ground
her bare feet tip-toed through
kangaroo grass and she wove
her hand into mine. She wanted
to talk art like 15-year-olds do
so I said something about Dali or Dada.
Water would have helped, that metal
tang easing the words in the mouth
but her neck was long, curved long
an open throat stretching toward me.
Her black dress shushed at my crotch
and that newness was lost as we twisted
around a rhythm unattainable
to people so young. But the dirt knew
and the stones knew that this hard
clasping tenderness would flood
a life as the blunders of a body
began in a heat so low down
bursting calamity into an ear.
The weight of another body
is welcome until it is on top of you
all its sticky traction, the sun
flaring as she toured my face in
the hope there was more to me.

H-O-M-E

Sound it out to me
sound out each part
to make it make sense.
Sound the drone of going
down gears on a column
shift, sound the shift
of gravel, the punch
of potholes and the long
exhale of a carport
holding off summer.

Sound the screen door
its petty clap
shutting the backyard
beef of *enough enough*.
Sound our hunger
on chipboard floors
bubbling with a need
for popped toast, sound
the sound of home again
sound it out to me.

Redesdale Road

I've come here now
when it is too late
to find anything to take
and make it back.

I've come for the children
thighs drenched
or low down
in cutting grass

chasing a father
that smoked nothing
but tobacco on his thumbs.
I've come for the ashes

in the bitter gales
that slap ground water
burping paddocks of toads.
If I find only a mother

at a pot belly stove
I'll take them and go.
The walls are thin
winter is inside now.

I've come here for this.

Looking at us as Leonardo, Donatello, Raphael and Michelangelo

In the face of every child
is a compass without north
a needle with no magnet

or arrow to show home.
The lines here run everywhere
but through us – a horizon

of parched weatherboard
a grid of unmarked roads.
Children kneel down, stoop

in the suits of superheroes
a mongrel band of four turtles.
We will wait an age

for our moment to hold
our hands with some clear
cause, but only one will

make a fist of hard
justice as villains run easy
in the world around us.

Mea culpa

How long could we stand the taste
of nickel from a 9-volt battery
pressed to the velvet of our lips?

As long as an afternoon
pinging golf balls
across the busiest street in town.

Why did we spend days sentencing snails
to spittle in the salt or pull frogs apart
until they were small sacks of limbs?

Because flung stones knew
no end when we plotted the flight paths
of magpies fever red in the eyes

when we chased lambs
until they were lost in the field.
Why do I stare at a wall

about a millimetre to the side
of you when you speak
to me of hard times?

Because this is the beginning
of what is required to see
loss on the inside of love.

Hills Hoist

At the end of aggregate
concrete is a glossed rotary
clothesline, its galvanised arthritis
tilt-snapping in the southerly.
It's a web of tines loose in
the winds we've waited for.
So up its crimped collars
we climb, ball and socket
crankshaft then crowning
we swing one-armed past cables
and wait for some underling
to grab on our heels, then spring
forward at our wild spurring.
Our centrifugal joy will splay
outwards, both of us will
look across this imperceptible
diameter in our lives
hear that rust shudder and know
briefly we are weightless.

Eye of the dog

if it leans towards me
I am in for it
forward on all fours
stiff and square
eyes searching for one
wrong twitch
the only scent I want
to leave is air
fear is enough
to let it believe
the world is its world
this fractured footpath
this stilted day
where a one-inch pitch
or an eye-to-eye meeting
could mean it's on me
rigid and striated
where skin will be split

Packed in front and back

Me, her and mum were shouldered on that bench seat when the tyre blew.
It was hard enough to have a red bomb when everyone else had Toyotas
let alone be broken down on a roundabout under a booming eucalypt.
So I slid down the cracked vinyl and that girlfriend looked sweet but still
while mum barked and popped the pitted boot for a jack and the will
for lug nuts. The hazards clicked fear into my heart, wrenching me
from my giddy footsies as mum ratchetted up that sedan shaking
its insides and clicking the stick shift like a chiropractor
finding the spot. In the rear my sisters teeheed a redness that fingered
up my neck and they tell that girl that our fire truck ruins everything
that our Falcon lets you know where we are from, that it is never
just as simple as dropping you and off you go.

The hours

I'll take what I can
small shifts, 4-6am.
In the winter it's fine
when dark lifts from the fields
when the world is nothing.
I like it under mist
when I pull on white boots
the hush of my gown
and eyes all sticky.
I'll go with my hands –
it's all that I've got.
I'll pluck those honey
feathers from boiled birds
hang them from a hook
faces flensed from bone
and my hide will soften
sting with this chemical
rash and its callus.
When I thumb the nub
of these scaly palms
I'll think of the hours
the click of my card.
I'll work all these years
with a grip that gets lumpy
these knuckled mitts,
their black nails
and the hours.

90s tribute remix

Blue Light Discos don't really have blue lights
nor many hometown cops dressed as cops.
Not here in the brick veneer of winter
in a Masonic Lodge where the hall is choofing
with Lynx Voodoo and Impulse Free Spirit.
On a stage, where no play has played
since the 60s, Poss and Morsey DJ a set
on their tip yard turntables. Cougar-
Mellencamp, Ace of Base and Roxette roll on
and because it's the country there is always
the Nutbush. Against a sea of teen sebum I walk
to the wall for anything but those moves –
an Egyptian cross-turn pivot and clap
a kick into space. When a hand reaches into mine
it fast becomes strip lighting and stairwell
the yeast breath of Bacardi. Tongues rasp as that ditty
about Highway Number 19 thunders into our echo.
And that song's unknowable Americanness makes
the cold chill through my coolest Hypercolour shirt –
no sign of heat when ready strangers kiss.

Hands

after Kwame Dawes' 'Your Hands'

No others have slid over me
warm with the heat of Tiger

Balm, with the focus of someone
intent on making a thing mend.

You always had a song as smooth
as skin still moist from dishwater

singing Que Sera Sera whatever will
be as you pulled back my forehead

until I looked like a saint again.
When I see your hands hardening

now I know they fold because
the work is no longer there

never at ease until the next child cries
or a man falters when he shouldn't.

Those hands must move
as they must, to the spilt mug

to the salt in the tears
the flaws within reach.

Trip to the pool

Outside the echo chamber
of a change room
sun spiked children
trample everything for water.

Pooling all their shivering
heat they leave concrete
ghosts suctioned from the perfect
underworld of Band-Aid soup.

Blue kneed and elbows gripped
they believe it's best to go
to ground, saying warm cement
is the *only way to survive.*

This is why we are different

It could be wood or some epoxy resin
but this small chin-pitched Mother of God
statue is gracefully watching, in complete
cooperation with her beatific calling.

From the backseat of our Hyundai Excel
we can see her faded cobalt gown
clipped in all safe, and her bare feet
more blocky than finely hewn art.

Mum the driver, ever the choir master
sings in part Tagalog, part English
about The Annunciation and Angel Gabriel
as this stiff idol of a woman tips over.

We shout *Mum this is crazy*
why is a sculpture getting a ride
but she is adamant that this week
Blessed Virgin Mary rides shotgun

up front, to be lifted to the front pew
of every downcast congregation.
Driving down High Street us kids
duck for our fucking lives

as the mute Nazarene's forehead
and its white skirt go on a 40km-an-hour
tour past all the unholy sanctums
in a teenager's country town life.

Begging for mercy (*Please stop*)
we find only more prayers to come
the pleats of her silent blue robe
her surety in the beauty of the hereafter.

Gorse

Sunlight be our master
water bog hop to us
dead cold soil is no
problem for tuft tops.
We re-spawn at each
beheading, power up
telekinesis, teleportation
is fine, any pixelation
of green works wonders.
Camouflage, subterfuge
a usurpation of cement
the stagger in crack
splits, fissures in redgum
sleepers or wherever there
is moisture warm enough.
Split ends under secateurs
we will bleed white loco
juice that sucks on skin
leaving red areoles.
We star ankles, nibble
a pricking constellation
leave a bloodlust
in those human eyes.
Die once, live twice
our zombie-stiff mass
spine sprogs, rebirths up
a pipe. We will sting
passers-by, open wide
shut on sighting, only to
gawp our acidic yawn
again to the power of two.

Subfloor

To taste
dust, its flour
grains pasting
the palate
clagging the lips.

To hear
a footstep turn
into a bullet
a mallet
thudding down.

To smell
what nothing
smells like, how
air so still goes
wet and falls.

To see
shins of light
sticks of freedom
squares of silence
napkins of hope.

To touch
the ruins of living –
femur, incisor, jaw –
the quiet balled sleep
an omen on emerging.

Crickets

They are fast maracas
crowing along summer.
In the warm world
nothing moves
this hedging air
a tremble among fat
rain, a rhythm of raw
rolling that a neighbourhood
porch sitter doesn't hear.
Stand up – everything still
veers, will become
water, a sub-molecular
tremor swinging one
wolf note, one hitch
we cannot fix.

The king

Today will it be the lone hand wrangler
or the Las Vegas ferris wheel?
Above his old vinyl head we'd drop
a pin that fine point parting static
scratched as summer sun until we heard
the big band blast or his late afternoon
croon under the flow of creek willows.
That quiver might have stopped
a Mississippi soldier or held girls
in the screaming section but
it's Elvis the elder that's the heart
of this high cholesterol matter.
That old fried chicken hamburger lickin'
heart freighted the weight of *thank you*
very much that clawing hand spinning
lights divining some closing
audience to watch sequins blaze.

Roadkill

All resolve is mowed down.
Finally they can tip their noses
to the sky, milk-eyed and scare-
crowed, crumbed and slope-lipped.
A wombat goes pop
forelegs turn brush-barrels
loaded with fermented style.
Four claws hold up a sun.
A dead-drunk Atlas is stiff-
armed, forked in mid waltz.
Our death shuttles zoom on
past the deer chambers, gore
spear, shear bone and cleft.
Buzzy mobflys stop and go
and proppy-legged ravens
craw around rib cage specials.
Bodies make perfect projectiles
a culvert stump, a crack of stick
on stick. The bumper belt of cars
learns to keep the wheel
dead straight. If the poor things
could please stop, stop, stop
pumping into our moonlight hug.

Dead eye

It took a lot less than first
thought to end a life
a stone cradled on the thumb
cocked under the index, thrown
with a bowlers' arm from deep
toward the swallow stopped
for a second among seedlings.

Collision was swift
here and the ever after.
In my hands its rosewood
body was soft as the under-
side of a foot, those wings
I tried to open again, always
tending towards shut.

Gunsmoke of a waif kitten

Heaped up with the kindling
I watched my mother go –
the thin case of her fur
diminishing from a warm body
to dim-lit waking. When it comes
the shovel head is cold.
Birth was never for me, nor
the circumstances of living.
I move deeper into the wood-
shed, a home to house spiders
and the diminishing

returns of hardwood joists.
Here among an unseen
world, the kids offer me
another mother's cool milk.
They'd have me sit and flicker
the small flame I felt once
in my throat, a heat I have
yet to sing: a *come, come here*.
They'd have me sit and open
the edges of their evenings,
have me give, instead of hiss

Coppice green

Demolition day

after Cornelius Eady's 'I know (I'm losing you)'

Have you ever put your palm
on the back of your mother's neck
and held it there as it all
came down?
She knows what this means –
her fingers denting my forearm.
The cattle tap on steel ramps
and the gear drops from Mack trucks
have stopped. I am a city person now
but up close the bypass still whines
across frosted paddocks
and the mud slung dams
and the Cyclone fence that keeps us
from the moorings of that first life.
I say to myself *I must remember all of this.*
Still the dozers go, dancing on
the sugar gums where my brother
clicked apart an ulna, where the rusty pins
of a pitchfork threaded his meta-
tarsals and he ran inside to her
in the steam of living
at a stove crowbarred by hard-hat
men and their vape-smoke.
She knows what this all means
but refuses to speak
or even look at the field pits
where the ewes were shot
where tiger snakes scrolled anger
and my father marched out there
absurd in gumboots and gaiters
to strike with the flat side
of a shovel the whipping force
of venom the smoulder of grass fire.

She knows that we are long gone
but what it meant was more than
the reverse alarms on a Caterpillar
more than the seethe of a shed cat
or the musk of empty sheep pens
or yabbies slatey in our pincers
socks silted from the urge to raid
every acre of what we had.
She knows my palm now means
something that is behind her
and by her and before her.
And I hate how I have never
put my hand on her
like this, until now.

Superb lifelike visuals

A small floorplan and everything else
big – like the 98-inch Smart TV
with quantum dots and a boofy couch –
turns this place into a 24-hr loungeroom
where my parents are not blinking.
Their hands don't orbit anywhere
near the other. Perhaps that's marriage –
people don't touch, but touch can't
work when Blu-Ray tickles burnt milk skin.
Sometimes I can edge a question in like
how is life in the hometown? And sometimes
there is an answer, like the meat works
is closing and a consortium has moved
in and the Filipino boys mum houses
are going to miss permanent residency.
Jeez mum, I say, that's a bombshell
but silence resumes, bar the jingle
snare and a thick-necked morning
show front man laughing at small
things which don't move a muscle
on their soft faces. If it were quiet
enough perhaps we could all move
closer, I mean it's a small place
I've been away and the murk
is still lurking around this room.

Blood moon

for Hugo

Lean in to me tonight.
Forget how I have hurt you.
The salve we are seeking
between us is nearby.
I'll pull you close, standing
in the grass wet
from night's dewlap
the sky clearing
just at the moment
our bodies prop
in the shadows of
a troughed out moon.
Prove we can join
in sketching dead suns.
Prove we can stay
in the cold now.
I'll stand where you say
so you can tip
an eclipse to your eyes
so you can see through
an umbra's lisle.
See something in
disinterested stars.

It arrives in my boy's hand

from the boundary of shadow
banding how we must live.
An open palm, across the blue
screen embalming night, says:
this one is for you, a note –
do not open this now
do not touch it until I leave
until I am far from here
so that I cannot see you.
It is for you, for your eyes
only, to make sense of.

Elegy after fight with my eldest

Thrown back in after
a three-day break from
the wild careen
of this domestic life
you and I meet again
in our sweet-timed squabbles
where sunlight stabs
across the afternoon
and air stampedes after
you have slammed the latch
so hard it makes glass loose
in its rectangular stillness.
I've played my part
lost sense of the right way
stood too tall too fast
breathed as if a hot sun
was really necessary
in this small room.
My other boy goes quiet
watching dust motes meeting
right in front of us
then veering away.
He waits with hush perseverance
learning to listen
to lit things being lost.

Somewhere I am here

I'm tired
of all this
waiting.
I've tried

and I'm tired
every day
a sway
I've tried.

I'm tired
of this body
a chump
I've tried

and grown tired
of starting
over again.
I've tried

the tired
mornings on
myself and
I've tried

to tire
nights out
each one asking
if I've tried.

*

I should be writing
but I am not I am
thinking about how

I will set my seedlings
in the nature strip
thinking about how

I will place every one
of those crisp stems
thinking about how

I will need to tend
and defend them
thinking about how

I am a passing hazard
a mark in the soil
thinking about how

I will stretch the earth
the scar I'll leave
thinking about how

*

given enough time
my two small boys
will return their figures

weaving
the edge of forest
given enough time

they will go ahead
or fall behind
find leading means

nothing to walking
slowly in the wake of
just stepping alone

given enough time
being together
will be like this –

me some midpoint
for their bodies drifting
given enough time

Looking at my son's birthday card to me

His drawing is a Texta scrawl of two circles
picket thin eyes, hair melting.
One is marked *Dad*, the other *Me*.
It strikes me I'm seeing something foundational
the creation story of his minor universe
which all life will eventually overgrow
cover in complications, fretworks of shade.
It's easy to forget the first principles of everything.
But this world of his is an undeviating motion
attentive to two bodies
that have never ever been apart.

Drowning with two kids

You find out water is fire
that it wants to burn
every bit of air
cloak your throat.
There are currents in words
arms fast becoming legs
slapping the sheen
of the world as it slips
through spangled hands.
Kids dog paddle
a chubby fierceness
in their faces pulling
us all down the acidic
search for a pontoon.
Among the invasiveness
everything that was clear
is now unsalted darkness.

Slide

Looking into the face of a plastic
stormwater drain, it feels like the end
of my life vomiting up chlorine
and children, a madcap kindness
spinning car tubes, the spume
of pleasure and expletives.
We wait in the cold line
our wet sternums concerned
at the complexities of water.
From four flights of steel
and rust, our stomachs wallow
when we reach that immense
gate sucking back its gulp
clear in the air it takes from us.
We squidge into race faces
and in the beginning it is slow.
Until the drop, then it all gives way
and we forget gravity, the density
of our bodies, the undulation of what
we are gets lost in the surging curve.
In nosedive blackout, the belly
of churn, we lurch our voices
to each other, the bowl
of lash and throw, and lean long
into breathing, speaking just
enough to know we are
somewhere near *here*.

The apiarist

Summer had gathered hot stones
and its ancient ache for inferno.
It sparked the chimney hive
into overdrive at the noon disc
that ticked everything up.
He said he'd wait until evening
business gets good
when the little ones stop surviving.
And slowly the sentries quieten
returning with the last baskets
of gold for a Queen's gilded bed.
Up the ladder he went, ascending
to a crown of wings, his leathered
legs veined in his smoke churning
blooms of termination.
Spatulating his way into sweetness
the catacombs of syrup-tenure
fell from the walls of brick
and he claimed this empire
smelt like charcoal, a carcinogenic
condiment you might taste once.
As night crowded in, its slow
darkness licked at the tang
of kerosene and honey
drawing a diaspora into its throat
viscose on bodies of the damned.

After Nick Cave's *Waiting for You*

The escarpment was dwarfing
when his fingers found
those familiar chords.
I pulled my young son closer
his hooded head pressed
to my chest, as if taking him
would hold us from Nick's
slow churning story of loss.

My child did not speak
just craned up higher
as if this song was another
curiosity from this curiously
suited man, but I knew
the imaginable reality Nick
had sat down to play.
Of the disappearance

of a body that had grown
to be part of your own
of an arm that could finally sling
across your shoulder
as a comrade's does.
Of eyes that could point blank
into yours and speak to you
as someone now equal.

In the honeyed twilight, Nick
sang it straight, perhaps so
I didn't need to, but it didn't stop
the tow of my arms, my cheek
moving to my boy's cheek
hoping I'd never have to drive
through the night and park
on a beach and say nothing at all.

Swimming lesson

(after 'The Swimming Lesson' by Jule Polkinghorne)

let's find our plunge   hold
hands   dunk us slow   then
bend us   among the ghosts
the swill of our domesticated
home bodies   let them slip
I'll shine for a minute longer
enough for you   to cup
the back of a knee   enough
to take a child   to the edge
& echo together   genuflect
then ask can I bow my head
to bear the black around us?

Salvage yard with children

Small voices say this place is sketchy
and when the old voice of the owner scraps
on about where used doors are, I listen
for a way through the goat trails
ride the swell and tide of car tyres
axle arms and an atrium of aromas
like demolition and spilt diesel.
Small voices say I want a stop-go sign
and a gouged Gunn and Moore.
That double French door slung
from a ceiling makes a middle-aged voice
say *bit Silence of the Lambs* and decades
of rain has turned the floor fishy.
The laminex bookshelves bulge
and the voice says again *step slowly
because the world still moves beneath you.*
There are doors buried here, secret
ways through the belly of the past
to a procession of Edwardian mantels
mouldy with teapots and light suppers.
We'd all held hands to start but
what I'm hanging onto now is detritus
and I'm still waiting for that nail
through a warm foot, for blood licking
through our blackened crust cut
by this place and its grey-damp weather
its teetering tetanus mounds.

On the rug

By chance we come together
in child's pose, on knees
and forearms our flanks finally
touching as our snouts are drawn
to the dog lying there, curling
the night inward. His breath
is open and we loosen into
that one holy interval in our day.
We have nothing he wants now
except our palms behind each ear
and when we do that he becomes
even more beautiful
lifting his crown so easily
as if he has reached that place again
only children and animals know.
And as all dogs have done
he stays his masters right there
frail in a moment a little less
slender than his own.

Hallelujah

The morning my father
in-law died, I put on
every cover I could find
of Leonard Cohen's *Hallelujah*
and vacuumed every bit
of dust and dead skin.

It wasn't that I loved Leonard
I just got thinking about if
there really is much difference
between versions of the one
story, whether there is another
way to hear a sad song about loss.

It wasn't that I loved Leonard
it was also that my boys sang
happiness into a cheerless tune
repeating an ancient word
that is partly about holiness
and partly about joy.

Coburg Leisure Centre

Water is most of the time static
like when you get whining rainfall
searching for the right frequency
on a radio but things never clear.
Voices wobble over the wavering
film until they find what they have
come for, stammering then shrill
into the ears, a shot of liquid.
I look to what I know and it's you
but all wet – you look like a newborn
again that underbite and your jaw
stretching white in your lap lane.
I recall us once lying skin to skin
that soft bread smell you had.
The voices keep tumbling over
wet concrete and thin walls.
Pools are polyglot and my eyes
are liars and the swimmer
that was beautiful underwater
is now just some stranger
when surfacing onto land.

Pass the special sauce

Sitting above our placemats
chewing fat over ageing
I say to you when arteries fill
I'll stent the contracting world.

It is not yet time to ground
the truth of how things really are.
Grandpa took his first steps today
echoing across a hospital's marble

the dog dreamed – its simple
skull pulsing with night flight.
On TV, the world wars again
and I say to you, angled

low from the kitchen table –
something will get sorted out.
Please son, outgrow this rust
belt belligerence and its guns.

Then you say we were all once
a tribe heading north together.
I say good, please let your life
coppice green, your plan

must be better than my own.
Though the reefs you never saw
have died, hang tough and grow
your beard deeper and darker

than your genes allow. Let's
thumb the rosellas on a label
the dimples in glass casing
homespun tomatoes and sugar.

You talk of holding babies
in your once baby arms, smelling
their molasses and unending gifts.
I say to you when an ice age comes

breathe warm on me, it will halt
the cold and the winds will not
wail but rather hum a song
that is still worth hearing.

Tooth Fairy

When I pulled your tooth
you wanted me to hold you.

It clicked lighter than
a pebble in the paw.

You smiled and blood laced
that first feeling of loss

the new emptiness in you.

Primer coat questions

My mind is between mice
either breaking their kiwi
fruit skulls, their fuzzy husks
the clicking of supple spines.
That day I was a genocidal killer
and usually I am not white
but today I am because concrete
leaves lime on me and so
does paint. It's a DIY invasion.
Plugged in, podcast poets
refer to their self or 'selves' as if
no-one else can get them
and if I'm being honest I'd say
I am confused too. *Aren't I just me?*
My dog can apparently look with love
the same love I have for him.
I need that now when I think
of my son and how I'm losing
him. Sure, we've connected over
mandolin chords – he can hear a C
when I can only hear fading echoes,
together we've rued how flies now bite.
Then I remember the song of stroking –
Up, Down Daniel Son, Uuup-dowwwn.
There are big questions for me
in the molars of storm clouds
things like *is there enough time*
to finish the thing I have started?
Is being part Pinoy making me good
at humidity? Maybe I will finally
meet my mother on her terms
as the world warms her barrio.
Does dark skin make me immune
to cancer? I paint on, straight

and conservative over taped edges
watching white bore into my fingers
turning those tan eddies into pale whorls
and I worry again about my son and his rat
tail and flat feet and double joints
and anaphylaxis and vague falsetto.
Am I just some cruel tight-faced
master slapping on strips of white?
The world as I remember will suck
the mother tongue from your mind
put it with all things that have gone.
How many coats are needed before you
can't see the grain? What will stop
the weather splitting timber to its core?

If

I had quiet
council with God

in that dim
cove I'd ask

why it was
all not left

still, why it –
this place – was

mucked about with.
Why was there

the need for
anything much more?

The day goes dark at the moment

I think of you, at four in the afternoon
when the street is stilling for the night
and cold lays down on the road
that blackens fast at this time of year.
An empty house can just happen
the nature strip pulling itself close
when it starts raining like it does
in the pines in British Columbia
like it did for Rambo in *First Blood*
when the sheriff sent dobermans
skidding over wet earth to find him.
No dogs bark here when it rains
and I wonder if the soil is moved by
wattles bowing their drenched gowns
pulling spectres of a storm across
my work shirt and desert boots
embossing me with a sky of soiled
canvas and spring letting go.
The birds hide somewhere
anywhere but right here, where a lake
forms on the lawn, the path turning
into mud that moves towards our home.
If I'd thought of you before I do
not now, because the rain comes again
dialling up its increments like when you
first find a song that sounds so fine.

Winds

Southerly

Wind that comes from another place –
a place where I do not know you
and you do not know me.
A place we have never held
the oblique of our bodies
the nape of our skulls.
This wind says *winter* – or I do –
coming from somewhere without
warmth, somewhere the cold
is never told, where the failings
in the world have remained.

Northerly

When the tropics swing thunder
hulks over our cold south,
buffalo grass stands to receive.
You have been gone some time now,
we wait until the days heal over
standing on lawn, dwelling on
further north. These winds pour
a mallee into us, eddy
a brief summer in our hair.
We smell the chest of you again
your heat close enough for now.

The untying

The look on his face tells me
this is important.
Not important in the way
that says something
grave or worldly has happened
but in the way that says
his small struggle is real.
For him, there is only so much
bitten nails can do
when the issue is hard
fused nylon and a double knot.
When he finally hands me
his shoe he keeps on watching.

Everyone who is defeated needs
to know how their victor ends up.
How on earth did you do this?
I don't know, it just got worse.
As my own fingers sting
from the force required
to pull apart that taut bind
I feel the same urge to give in.
But when it comes apart
at last, we breathe and open
the bloody thing up
and repeat the same
mundane loops again.
Remember, too much
tightening is too much.

Bubbles

Over tree root and claypan
by a detritus creek, rope
swinging between sewer
and silurian cliff
I push the small of one
boy's back, going
then returning in pirouettes
above the swivel of water.

Each landing is a stretch
a toe-hold on certainty
above old axles and effluent.
Upon stillness we crouch
pull bindis from our socks
till the scales of hot coals
flare in the brown tomb
of that bottomless confluence.

There, the tinsel of trimming
the jacket shimmer of fish
forming a loose S in the currents
pulsing from erosion, looking
 – without ideas or impulse –
for something bigger, better
than what is here right now.
This goldfish could be

the ultimate wonder
a nonchalant comet
of copper coins
het up by fire
in these crawling urban dregs.
The size of a man's forearm
and buffed bold as Fanta
it drifts in curtains of ooze

empty faced and draping hope
or mercy, its perfect rim
beneath the earth's undercuts
raising a cup of quiet, seeking
pure air or an answer
joining us together in one
circular question – *for what
would you like to be forgiven?*

Streetlights slur vision

Walking for the weak

1
Before we start, the dog is airing
the grey scar of castration.
We take one step, then hit wet heat
and mozzies feathering in a puddle.
Rain skirts further south
strong arm in pre-workout.
An old woman greets us
in moccasins and nightie
pigeons break the exchange
scattering Zorro swashbuckler
sounds as the dog goes stiff.
Deep grass makes me nervous
streamer heads barbing my legs.
Snakey vibes all round today, so
we middle path it like moderates.
Fly balloons explode to the side
his nose jerk says *death-now-go*.
At a drain pond crickets continue
to sip summer and Pobblebonks joke
So a Martian walks into a Tiki bar.

2
Some people still live remotely
straight-backed, lap topping the porch.
They are missing something – toad
rachets, viridian visors of dragonflies.
Their flung crucifixes silver the brown
creek scum and a waterlogged Princess
Pony toy sludges on the sidewalk.
Fairy tales are no good in floods.
Losing part of your body is exhausting
and my desexed boy pants on, limp-
hopping under graffitied ghosts

and hot clouds clenched in boulders.
One plane burrs ahead of a storm
but we miss the symbolism
looking at the mould everywhere
and tree wind sounding like rain
casuarinas whispering they missed out.
Groundwater mushes into his paws
and I cuss the mud again, the slit
earth and its failure to hold.

3
A young couple linen up their love
it's the weather for it, but something says
it's a drenched thing, they look happy.
Wet Labradors smell a fresh wound
the heaped salt of hurt, the tear
of loss. We pass a Pomeranian
that follows us without thought
before meeting its range and turning.
Three muggy couches crumble outside
the hippies' house, their rushing
Neo-Mastiff doing steely-blue beautiful.
One of the hippies can't look up
from a doom scroll – seems
every free spirit is a slave.
This season is strange, sun wink
road stretch, weeds divvying up
to go swing dancing in the street.
We walk on, sore as each step is
four little to one big, the dank split
of discomfort marked everywhere.

Byron Baes

Jade faked a selfie, just
him and Kim Kardashian
cat eyes pinned and sleek.
Outside it is all white
white clothes, white sand
white feet under fake
tan and white hair sometimes
flush on skids of sunburn.
Sound healing helps, really
cleanses, allows these creatives
a chance at world peace.
Are they actors or for real?
It's hard to tell, they are so
earnest in ways Hollywood
actors can't be.
Human nature is so trippy –
are we mean deep down
or is love everywhere?
For an hour, this world is
real, because Byron Bayers
are real and Gold Coasters
are not – they dish dirty looks
like they are on parole.
Linen and dream catchers
get you closer to God
or Mother Earth or Buddha.
You and me, day ted now.
They have it out – duck lips,
no-likes, the non-mentions
saying they couldn't make it
when really they could.

Urban sprawl

on the sappy side of pine paling
paddocks crackle underfoot
tyre piles spiral before striking.
arriving aspirants live large –
gloss-tiled splash-backed faces
laminate smiles with rectangular
catalogues of homesteads
and limewashed floors.
could this be all we ever wanted?
over the boundary cockies
once ran cattle, then sheep on native
grasses, curlew ground and basalt.
across that fence is frontier now
for faux Georgian tenure
and double-breasted suit men
thinking at right angles over
the fault lines of hillock
and tiger snakes whipped open.
this estate's polystyrene jumps
the wire and bolts gowns trailing
plastic, sketching the northerlies.
arterial roads tune on redgums
glum in their diminishing domain.
could this be all we ever wanted?
baffled as the red tiles come on –
the stacked shields of a squadron.

Single front terrace

Sun fingers vines
through cracks
in a former corner
of architrave and cornice.
Ants rewild a wall
trace a braille on
the tea stained
map of render.
For years this house
slumped into earth
suffering a one-sided
stroke while the other
lived in the lamplight
of break ups and going
down on strangers.
When we left
mildew came with us
a damp rising
through our cottons
a dust tracing
on our lungs.

Tachyglossidae

A ripple in the world –
the prince crowned
not in kingdom but spiked
with grunt work, the fist
of muscle flexing into
a kinder earth than here.
Its rump treads a crackle-
pop of leaf litter blanched
for burning, the expired
air, searching for something
more divine than water.
If I could dig into secrets
contract into the heat
of wasted things
would I stay armoured
or would I run
full of knowing?

This is what happens

Day broke off quick
the white pits opened
glow-zooming through
the hard darkness.
Those rectangular eyes
were awoken when the sun
wavered in its repeat
argument about being.
A half-life began
the slack-jaw response
as the unsheathed light
fell on a glazed face.
That slow-moving
chain we followed blind-
sided us with a pole.
A chest became a screen
for jolty searching
scrolling for answers
to unending questions.
Inside the timber boxes
more white boxes
were dawning.
People were thumb
struck, double tapping
half walk-stumbling.
It is night now for everyone.
But it used to be street
strolls, the quiet
just you and me.

Carcass

cow prongs high noon
the brahmin tail a dial
for shadow at a boab's base
there's the tap root and its water
or lack of it in the flint and grit
ears hear no noise bar
ringing of sun splinters
through parchment thin as porcelain
pinging high and low whine
blowflies winking green
over a clear cerulean dome
hipbone ridgelines to jawbone
sinkhole amphitheatre of innards
the locked out eye slump
clacking ball in socket and sun nicks
off west the hide hangs canvas
tough sails sagging flat for now

Thumbsucker

While lying on a full body chair
staring into operating lights
there pops the face of my mellow
orthodontist, Keanu, telling
me to let go of my thumb sucking
to look directly at a picture
of a moon rising over three wolves.
Has he just smoked a spliff?
The way he is talking is like you do
when drunk or stoned
each phrase a careful placement
to avoid goosestepping in sand.
But every word Keanu speaks
is a soft dimple on my heartbeat.
I stay the course with my gnarly
man as he says *the more relaxed*
we are the deeper we will go.
Then his voice starts filling
my feet and legs and his drifting
unplaceable naivety is something
I am taking very seriously now.
For it seems this nice dude has
sorted all my dim-witted confusions.
I shut my eyes faithfully
when he urges me to *find*
your power animal.
And when I imagine a fawn
munching in a forest clearing
Keanu is also there in his white
coat and faint Jesus beard
smelling like echinacea.
It is unclear if he is now
my power animal purring
low with his Cali drawl, pure

in his belief I shouldn't fix myself
that life is just a mix
of guesswork and hoping
and living without an answer.

Suburban aubades

1
There is a Coles trolley
silent on the nature strip
reminding us that at night
there is a city shiver
the grin of youth
opening under force

2
Hold people in long enough
they'll let their dogs out
to shit on every unwalled
patch of green wedge.
Look down – there
the thin slit of undervoice.

3
Last night's street lore –
true bitch I have your fucking phone.
A mob of beards with a gobful
of slag and chipped teeth move
to stun a face with a winter fist
chops that snarl flesh and bone.

4
The pardalote and its comma
of chroma falls hard
its knuckle of skull bare
in a tangle of enmity
the noisy miner tasting rage
and blood within its range.

5
The point of the fox
is that you never see
the fox, when it comes
it goes and is no more
than a stream
of fox over fences.

6
A child tries to cry
in secret, to independently
sit against the wind outside
the window, learning
that one day life will be
lived without you.

7
Think hard, think
how your hand of all places
is a sidewalk the Eastern
Spinebill could choose
to land and maybe call you
something like *still*.

8
When I wake I take
one of your feet in my clasp
and I close over your instep.
Your eyes wait for mine
while I search the day
for light that says start over.

Evander

He was a self-made heavy-
weight bulking on clay pots
of trapezius to a six-foot frame.
All along he said he wanted
to show how good guys can
make it with God's grace.
You can't always charge life
like a pit bull branded
so when Tyson stormed
with his small stance and simple
solutions, the Real Deal Holy-
Field had the feet to dance
with savagery in satin shorts.
How does temperament see
terror and win, when eyes
swell to pin cushions and skin
slicks to foam? An ear goes missing
on canvas, what was there is now
his foes in an appetite for torsos.
An engorged heart beats full
to the edges of its red frame
and no one seeks to see
if the man slumped is only
a corner of blood or
merely muscle unmoved.

Fog dream

When I found you
on a landing you'd done
all you could to stop
the blackest wind
our backs had ever known.
All night it had come
just for us, never stopped
reaching with stone hands.
When you found a way
to let all your feathers go
I watched as the warm thing
inside you grew and flew up
those ever-descending stairs.

Joey

Feet tips no more
than rosebuds, skin
as thin as membrane.
Inside this newborn
ringtail pulses bitumen
warm from summer's hell.
Gumnut eyes sightless
black ears folded
there is no mother
now as threadbare
noose of tail lets go.
What am I to do?
Give milk, cup
it dry in muslin?
Thimble head
bowed as a buttock
that puce bruise
on concrete would
take just one boot heel
to end a vellum paper skull.
But I don't, blister eyes
are blind to all universes
still as a baby's fist.
I'll mercy those who can
see frequencies in the light.
All the earth starts
as a wrinkle, a purse
of hope holding murmurs
contracting and unravelling
the strands of the day.
At some point I should
help, the argument
for life worming right there
but what could I ever really do?

Put its soft wild
pound in my pocket?
Place its unlacing
song on my palm?

After Agnes Martin

Moon crosshairs a window, bullseyes its crucifix on glass, stitching
    the scent of something pure.
A painter on hiatus loses nothing. If they wait for that simple mark
    pinpricked in the mind
the hands will recall the right proportions of titanium and shale and
    the walls will become water
the ground renewed in a dust of grey gloss, until they look up and the
    light has gone.

Dodgy lot

Streetlights slur vision
with billboards and Smith Street awnings.

2 am beers after a gutful of blokey
rev-ups, a skinful of eyeing.

Us boys are really lost –
the night is delicious

and some of us talk
to the stars as if we mean it.

I've been sampling stares
breathing deep against heartburn

in a neon-fuzz world.
Each ruthless bite is sustenance:

my breath on the innocent
the lurk beneath a jaw

serrated lust memory
and the taste of another.

Signed Planet Earth

after 'Signed Planet Earth', by Julie Field

Look long enough, there is Gauguin
in a flank, searing tar prints emerald
under heat. Porcelain pencils a hairline
crack, then clicks together the uptrend
slit across a muzzle. At the dock is a dove
clucking grey hope above the mottles
of cancer. Sizzle and streak, this colt
keeps bolting, mustang musk floating
legless on infernos, craters of carbon
barrel loaded over choked ground.

Prodigal people

The morning is unkempt as
if the life lived before the world
stopped had been remembered
on all the accelerators of every
early rising Isuzu and HiLux.
The cold hands of hi-vis
warriors wring, inside 7-11s
paying a dollar for a machine
coffee and standing under strip
lighting like imperfect drifters
in Hopper's diner at dusk.

Reverberation is memory
and trains bawling on the light
are only cattle in a sale yard.
You can feel the world's
jitter this time in the body
of the roads moaning again
to the heat of humans moving.
Earth is opening and closing
after a year absent from its
prodigal people, its one great
creation gone but come again.

Jellyfish pastoral

Call me a loose lung
call me an open bloom
with an ocean
moving through it.
Call me a bowl
with only the blow
of moon-strike.
I cannot name myself
any more than you can
name the constellation
of feelings as you pass
a place where you lost love
(or where you found it).
Under the quake
of water everything
is clear except what I take
and what I leave behind.
I find nothing now
only the current below
and the passing of O-
shaped mush like mine.
If you see me flung ashore
clipped lace threading
press me as you must.

Spearfisher

After standing as a statue
black as the swells
of this choppy ocean
you push into the dark
down to the channels
of limpets bejewelling
avenues that now crumble
with the touch of a glove.

Descending from the whorl
of the world's voltage
your barbs hum the upswells
of green light and with legs
swaying like wave-swoon
the weight belt takes you down
to where you hope there
is life enduring a maelstrom.

You heard that in the past
a dull patch on the sand
meant meat, that your rubber
mask could track death
and your white eyes
could snare open
let the air of the hunt
spiral in the incoming tide.

But the mariners then
and the mariners before
who howled from boats –
club thugged and bladed –
oiled up the beach with blood.
Now kids sit in too hot
rockpools, popping algae
honing dead husks of Dog

Whelk and Turban Snail.
Are there any more
voices down there
on the floor, in the brine
and the spume, circling
your skin as you strain
to reach the bottom
of your cold patrol.

Home range nocturne

Somewhere up on the hill, Sellotape
straps carnations to street saplings
there are big painted letters on the road's
camber where the boy was pack hunted
and his stabbed heart lost its air, hardening
from a thin glow to flecks of tar.
I never walked that pavement's buckle
because I turned before his loose-leaf shrine
and the boy with pools at his feet stayed
out of reach under a slice of streetlamp.

As I went on, words jabbing my tongue
were *depletion* and *squander* and *waste*
they covered the field of this wine
dark morning where I walked my pup
in rags of night, starting at every Frog-
Mouth landing and leaving with its haul.
If the words turned then to *absence*
there was surely something present
bopping between tallgrass, parting
pond reeds, the vixen's pelt flaming up

embankments loose with clay stone.
And when the blades of its eyes flashed
strobic to my gut, its stainless steel
unblinking, its trot struck out toward us.
I waited, watching as my dog (with no wild
left in it) had no sense that dying
has a definitive snick and downwind the pad
of predation came calm, two fox stars
meant only for those caught seeking.
So I stayed my right to bloody an animal

the word I longed for then was *question*
asking each flare of hair, each twitch-wire
what is the value of running or staying
when the whoop of a killer comes.
And that thick arm of fire-tail drifted out
then in in the sparked air between, turning
to find another tear in world, staying low
to the ground and spiriting towards that hill
drawn to something silent before light
before the day's promise and its peril.

Acknowledgements

Thank you to the editors of the following publications where earlier versions of these poems have appeared:

'Coburg Leisure Centre' and "Drowning with two kids" appeared in *Swim Meet Lit Mag*. 'Prodigal people', 'Hills Hoist' and 'Mea culpa' appeared in *Antithesis*. 'Origin story' appeared in *Rochford Street Review*. 'Blood moon' appeared in *Sunday Mornings by the River*. 'Gunsmoke of a waif kitten' and 'Dodgy lot' appeared in *Mantissa Poetry Review*. 'Trip to the pool' and 'Gorse' appeared in *Suburban Review*. 'Pass the special sauce' was shortlisted in the ACU Poetry Prize 2022. 'Joey' appeared in *Cordite*. 'Salvage yard with children' appeared in *Westerly*. 'Home range nocturne' was shortlisted in the Montreal Poetry Prize 2022. 'Signed Planet Earth' and 'Swimming lesson' were published as part of the Queensland Poetry's Ekphrasis Prize 2022. 'Primer coat questions' and 'The apiarist' appeared in *foam:e*. 'On the rug' appeared in *Meniscus*. 'Superb lifelike visuals' appeared in *Berlin Lit*. 'Packed in front and back', and 'Suburb aubades' appeared in *Nighthawk Literature*. 'Bubbles' was shortlisted in the 2023 Ada Cambridge Poetry Prize.

My poem 'Thumbsucker' borrows from the general tenor of Keanu Reeves's performance in the film *Thumbsucker*. Similarly, as is clear from its title, my poem 'After Nick Cave's Waiting for You' is heavily invested in the listening experience of that song.

Thank you to Terri-ann White, Emily Stewart, Ross Gillett, Debi Hamilton, David Francis, Mary Jones, Zenobia Frost, Izzy Roberts-Orr, Andy Jackson and Simone King for their valuable input and encouragement.

About Upswell

Upswell Publishing was established in
2021 by Terri-ann White as a not-for-profit
press A perceived gap in the market for
distinctive literary works in fiction, poetry
and narrative non-fiction was the motivation.
In her years as a bookseller, writer and then
publisher, Terri-ann has maintained a watch
on literary books and the way they insinuate
themselves into a cultural space and are
then located within our literary and cultural
inheritance. She is interested in making books
to last: books with the potential to still be
noticed, and noted, after decades and thus
be ripe to influence new literary histories.

About this typeface

Book designer Becky Chilcott chose
Foundry Origin not only as a strong,
carefully considered, and dependable
typeface, but also to honour her late
friend and mentor, type designer Freda
Sack, who oversaw the project. Designed
by Freda's long-standing colleague,
Stuart de Rozario, much like Upswell
Publishing, Foundry Origin was created
out of the desire to say something new.